THE ART OF WAR
FOR EXECUTIVES

THE ART OF WAR FOR EXECUTIVES

Donald G. Krause

A Perigee Book

A Perigee Book
Published by The Berkley Publishing Group
A division of Penguin Putnam Inc.
375 Hudson Street
New York, NY 10014

Copyright © 1995 by Donald G. Krause
Book design by H. Roberts
Cover design by James R. Harris
Cover illustration by James Barkley

First edition: February 1995

Published simultaneously in Canada.

The Penguin Putnam Inc. World Wide Web site address is
http://www.penguinputnam.com

Library of Congress Cataloging-in-Publication Data

Krause, Donald G.
        The art of war for executives / Donald G. Krause. —1st ed.
           p.   cm.
        "A Perigee book."
        ISBN 0-399-51902-5 (pbk. : alk. paper)
        1. Management. 2. Leadership. 3. Success in business.
4. Sun-tzu, 6th cent. B.C. Sun-tzu ping fa. I. Title.
HD38.K688   1995
658.4—dc20   94-29606
                                                  CIP

Printed in the United States of America

30 29 28 27 26 25 24 23 22 21

To Susan Ruth Bradshaw, Rebecca Anne Krause and Elizabeth Lorraine Krause

Acknowledgment

I would like to thank Dr. Bob Shively of the Babcock Graduate School of Management, Wake Forest University, for his assistance over the years, but particularly for supporting this book during its critical early stages. Bob has been associated with the Babcock School, as a professor of organizational behavior and as dean, for over twenty years. He is due a large part of the credit for the school's fine program and glowing national reputation.

I would also like to thank Dr. Chang Miao, principal of the West Suburban Chinese Language School in Villa Park, IL. Dr. Miao translated the original Chinese text that formed the basis for my interpretation. Dr. Miao has also given me the kind of insight into the Chinese culture and character that can only come from a person who was born and educated in China.

THE ART OF WAR
FOR EXECUTIVES

Introduction

Sun Tzu lived in Northeastern China 2500 years ago, about the same time as the famous Chinese philosopher, Confucius. Sun Tzu, and his father before him, were considered experts in military strategy due to their many victories on the battlefield. While there is no direct evidence that Sun Tzu actually wrote down his own thoughts, about 100 years after his death the great Chinese warlord Cao Cao carefully annotated a text on military strategy that was a compilation of Sun Tzu's teachings. Cao Cao's overwhelming success in battle using Sun Tzu's methods (he eventually united the whole of China) subsequently created great interest in the material. Over time, several successful military leaders have attributed their victories to Sun Tzu's principles. Most notable of these in very recent times was Mao Tse-tung. In addition, because the wisdom contained in the text applies to so many business and political situations, Sun Tzu is now studied and used by leaders throughout the world, but particularly in Asia.

Warfare is one of the more common events in the history of man. Because of its importance to survival, warfare has been studied carefully. The factors that contribute to success in war are fairly well understood. Fundamentally, success in war, as well as in business, is based on leadership. Other factors—information, preparation, organization, communication, motivation, and execution—also contribute to success, but the effectiveness of these factors is entirely determined by the quality of leadership provided.

Sun Tzu's central idea is that battles or competitions are won by the organization or person who, first, has the greatest competitive advantage and who, second, makes the fewest mistakes. Competitive advantage can be provided by many factors including superior manpower, superior position, superior execution, and innovation. Competitive advantage is readily understood by most people in business. But competitive advantage is not the determining factor in success. It is people who fight and win battles. And the most important person in the battle is the general.

According to Sun Tzu, the ideal general wins the war before the fighting begins. He does this in two ways: first, he develops his character over time; second, he creates a critical strategic advantage. In Chinese philosophy, character is the foundation of leadership. People with superior character become superior leaders. But a general's character cannot be developed overnight. Hence, people who want to lead must cultivate the characteristics of leadership over a long period of time. A general gains a critical strategic advantage by placing his organization in a position where it cannot be defeated and waiting for the enemy to give him an opportunity to win. He does this by managing information. An ideal general makes no mistakes. An ideal general is patient. An ideal general is inscrutable.

The Natural Organization:
Sun Tzu's Model for Effectiveness

Sun Tzu's army is modeled on what can be termed a "natural organization" model. Natural organizations have three characteristics. First, they exist to serve a defined purpose. The term of their existence corresponds to the time required to accomplish their purpose. Second, they are information-centered. Natural organizations seek and use data as a basis for action. They avoid unwarranted opinion and conjecture, choosing to deal with uncertainty by estimating reasonable probabilities. Third, natural organizations are completely flexible and totally adaptable. They respond quickly and effectively to changes in their environment that affect their ability to serve their defined purpose.

A clear and familiar example of a natural organization is the ant colony. Ant colonies have survived for hundreds of millions of years virtually unchanged. This is a record of accomplishment that is hard to top. The ant colony exists solely for the purpose of providing food and shelter for its members. Once successful in this purpose, it does not seek to expand its domain by acquiring, say, a nearby beehive or getting into another line of business.

The ant colony is totally information-centered. Members of the organization constantly seek information about sources of food for the colony. They quickly and efficiently transmit useful information to others in the organization.

The ant colony is totally flexible. Based on its need for food and shelter, the colony will quickly change its location and methods to take advantage of any opportunity discovered by a member.

Unfortunately, ant colonies have often been used as a model of extreme regimentation. As a result, direct comparisons to human organizations may not be appropriate on all levels. However, for the purpose of example and illustration, ant colonies can teach people a great deal. Further, since human beings do not seem to have the same type of narrow genetic programming, perhaps our species can enhance the strengths and reduce the weakness of the ants.

Sun Tzu begins chapters 7 and 8 by noting that the commanding general must be authorized by the ruler of the country to form an army to wage war. Sun Tzu's armies came into existence to serve defined purposes. They were created in response to specific, definite threats or opportunities. Presumably, these armies were disbanded after the threat or opportunity had passed. In this respect, Sun Tzu's armies resemble temporary project teams formed to design and construct large-scale systems in modern business settings. These temporary teams gather together resources to accomplish a defined set of objectives. Once the defined objectives have been accomplished, the team goes out of existence. The temporary project team concept has been so successful that it is being proposed by modern management theorists as the organizational model for the future.

Sun Tzu's army is also information-centered. Sun Tzu notes that superior commanders succeed in situations where ordinary people fail because they obtain more timely information and use it more quickly. The fundamental activities of an information-centered organization are gathering, processing, using, and giving out information. The leaders of information-centered organizations view all organization functions as information-driven. Hence, they increase organizational effectiveness by increasing the speed and improving the quality of information use by the people in the organization. Much like the newer computer chips, information-centered organizations create a greater number of channels to move information faster. They also reduce system overhead by reducing unnecessary intramural data requirements (e.g., interoffice memos, unused reports). They increase system response by obtaining more and higher-quality information; by training organization members to use information properly; by ensuring that organization members have quick access to data and allowing them to make and execute informed decisions based on information; and by efficiently transmitting information to organization members and outsiders. Information centricity is also a major tenet of modern organization theory, particularly theory associated with Total Quality Management (TQM).

In chapter 1, Sun Tzu challenges us to consider everything before taking action. He suggests that we should evaluate critical factors in the competitive situation to determine which party has the highest probability of winning. Although the modern science of probability and statistics was not known in Sun Tzu's time, the idea of assessing relative probabilities of specific outcomes of actions was well understood. Understanding probabilities and reducing the impact of unknown events were fundamental to Sun Tzu's thinking. Understanding probabilities and reducing the impact of unknown events also underlie the improvement methods advocated by W. Edwards Deming, Shigeo Shingo, and others.

A primary facet of oriental philosophy is the idea that the universe is constantly changing. To survive, human beings need to be flexible and adaptable in response to these changes. Natural organizations are completely flexible and adaptable. They structure themselves according to the requirements imposed by their objectives and the shape of the environment. Like water, they flow around obstacles and challenges, always seeking to follow the most effective path. Like water, they are essentially formless. They respond quickly and adapt readily to changing circumstances. If this description sounds familiar, it is because "continuous change" and "continuous improvement" are the heart of the Japanese management revolution.

Sun Tzu's model for effective organizations could come from one of today's management journals. His "natural organization" exists to serve a defined purpose; it is information-centered; and it is flexible. These three characteristics appear among those commonly associated with the most successful organizations existing now.

Sun Tzu's Principles of Success

For most people and organizations, today's battlefields are not physical places that can be located on a map. Today's battles occur within the minds of those who comprise the constituents of an organization, or within an individual. Organizational constituents include customers, employees, stockholders, politicians, news reporters, suppliers, virtually anyone who comes into contact with the organization. Individual constituents can include associates, superiors, clients, advisors, family and friends, in addition to the constituents of the organizations that employ or are served by the individual. Organizations and individuals win and lose on this battlefield based on how effectively they manipulate the perceptions and opinions of constituents.

Today's battles are information battles because information determines both perception and opinion. Those who use information weapons effectively, both to attack and to defend, will win. Those who do not will lose. Sun Tzu's ancient wisdom for fighting traditional battles applies equally well to fighting information battles.

The essentials of Sun Tzu's wisdom can be captured in ten short principles:

SUN TZU'S PRINCIPLES
1. Learn to fight
2. Show the way
3. Do it right
4. Know the facts
5. Expect the worst
6. Seize the day
7. Burn the bridges
8. Do it better
9. Pull together
10. Keep them guessing

These ten principles form the foundation for competitive success. Learn them well! (See Appendix for expanded discussion of these principles.)

Organization of Text

The traditional format of Sun Tzu's *Art of War* contains thirteen chapters. This text retains the thirteen-chapter format. The original text reads like notes gathered from a series of informal discussion sessions. Although each chapter discusses a somewhat different aspect of warfare, the material is highly interrelated. The book does not flow smoothly from one subject to another; rather, it jumps around quite a bit. Only chapters 12 and 13 ("Attacks by Fire" and "Gathering Intelligence") deal strictly with one subject.

There are actually two interpretations of Sun Tzu contained in this book. The first, and major, interpretation is designed to help the modern business reader use the material in everyday business situations. The philosophy underlying the major interpretation comes from three major sources. The first source is Sun Tzu and the many commentaries on his work. The second source is the ideas of modern business thinkers (Tom Peters, Peter Drucker, Warren Bennis, and many others). The third source is the writings of military strategists (Helmuth von Moltke, George S. Patton, and J.F.C. Fuller) on the principles of success in battle. Sections of the major interpretations are numbered for easier use and discussion.

A second interpretation is contained in the insets that appear periodically throughout the text, easily distinguished by their design. The insets give the reader a flavor for the original text of Sun Tzu, which contains a great deal of obscure language and Chinese idiom. The insets contain only the more important parts of each chapter. Taken together, the two interpretations in this text provide the reader with the substance and flavor of Sun Tzu in such a way that it can be used in today's business environment.

Author's note: The inclusion of brief passages from a literal translation of the original text has been included to let the reader see the differences between this contemporary interpretation of Sun Tzu's wisdom and a literal translation of his writing.

Estimates

Sun Tzu said:
War is the most important aspect in the survival of the nation. It is the way of existence and non-existence. It cannot be studied too much.

Therefore, we estimate using five principles and calculate our strategies. Then, we judge our course of action. Of the five principles, the first is called *Tao* (way); the second is called *Tien* (heaven); the third is called *Dee* (earth); the fourth is called *Gian* (leadership); and the fifth is called *Far* (law).

Conquerors estimate in their temple before the war begins. They consider everything. The defeated also estimate before the war, but they do not consider everything. Estimating completely creates victory. Estimating incompletely causes failures. When we look at it from this point of view, it is obvious who will win the war.

I  Planning

I-1

Competition is a matter of vital importance to the executive. Competition determines who advances and who retreats, who succeeds and who fails, who profits and who loses, who lives and who dies. The only true battlefield of business is the mind of your constituents. Every executive has constituents who must be served— those people you serve directly, for instance, your superiors and personal clients, and those people you serve indirectly through your organization's products and services. The cumulative impact of competitive actions enhances or deteriorates your power and influence. It is essential that your competitive actions be carefully planned and properly executed.

I-2

Appraise your plans for competition using five basic factors. Assess yourself and compare your competitors to determine the best course. Consider everything.

I-3
The five factors are: character; climate; structure; leadership; and information.

I-4
Character means the essential purpose—the spirit—of an individual or organization. Character influences how your constituents feel about you and your products; character determines whether constituents believe they are in harmony with your goals and objectives. When constituents share your spirit, they will follow your lead. They will buy your products. They will help you achieve your goals.

I-5
Climate refers to the impact of general business conditions and political culture on the competitive situation. To be effective, competitive actions must be conducted in the appropriate climate.

I-6
Structure is the way work is organized and managed. This is separate from the way people are led. Considering structure includes evaluating how you or your organization are financed; how well you and your employees are trained; how you develop your skills and how your organization develops its products and services; how well you and your organization employ technology and human resources; how flexible or inflexible, responsive or unresponsive, effective or ineffective, are your policies and procedures. Structure determines the basic capabilities of an individual or an organization.

Structure also includes fashion, technology, labor and materials, barriers to entry, key personnel, financial structure, and other external factors related to your performance in the marketplace. The interaction of these factors determines how easy or difficult it is to enter and dominate a market.

I-7
Because leadership comes from within, leadership flows from the attitudes and abilities of individuals. Organizational leadership is the aggregate of the attitudes and abilities of the key executives. Leadership can be assessed in terms of seven factors: self-respect, purpose, accomplishment, responsibility, knowledge, "laddership," and example.

I-8
Information means getting facts—timely, accurate facts—about the reality of conditions and circumstances in the competitive situation. Nothing in competition is more important than obtaining facts! Information also means giving out perceptions. Perceptions are facts and fiction that move your competitors and constituents where you want them.

I-9
Every executive has heard of these five factors. Those who master them will win; those who do not will lose.

I-10
When considering competitive strategy, carefully assess your plans and gather information using the following questions.

I-11

Which executive creates enthusiasm and cooperation among his employees and associates? Which organization creates enthusiasm and cooperation among its customers, executives, employees, suppliers, and other stakeholders? Which executives practice leadership according to the seven principles? Which executive is more favored by the current political climate? Which company is more favored by current economic policies and conditions? Whose strategy is able to influence more factors in the marketplace? Whose employees are better organized? Where is innovation truly encouraged?

I-12

Which executive is better trained? Which organization has the better trained executives, employees, customers, and suppliers?

I-13

Which executive builds people? Which organization truly rewards merit and encourages personal growth?

I-14

Using the answers to these questions, anyone can predict which plan has the greater chance of success.

I-15

The executive who heeds this advice is sure to succeed. Such a person should be placed in a responsible position. The executive who disregards this advice will fail. Such a person should be dismissed.

I-16
Taking into account the assessments already discussed, an executive must create plans for competitive actions which allow him to leverage his particular strengths within his organization and leverage the strengths of his organization in the marketplace. By competitive actions, I mean actions that bring an individual or an organization into conflict with other individuals or organizations. Leveraging your strengths gives you a competitive advantage.

I-17
All competitive advantage is based on effective execution of plans. Poor execution ruins superior plans. Superior execution saves mediocre plans. Further, superior execution can make more effective use of innovation and information. Surprise your competitors with your willingness and ability to adapt and change.

I-18
Therefore, constantly seek new approaches and methods, seek new market segments and different customers. Even with successful products look for new uses among old customers and new customers among those not considered before.

I-19
Keep your good name and your superior reputation before those who determine your future. Keep the quality and value of your products in the minds of your customers. Keep your customers' needs uppermost in your mind.

I-20

Draw constituents to you with the exciting promise of better service and more profit based on using your products. Dominate your marketplace with excellence.

I-21

In circumstances where your competitor is strong, develop innovative products and services. Look for indications of constituent dissatisfaction. Move quickly to meet needs. Where your competitor is weak, emphasize the advantages of your products. Look for better ways to serve.

I-22

Confuse your competitors with constant innovation and superior service. Innovation is the one weapon which cannot be defended against.

I-23

When your competitor is arrogant, be humble. Find out why he is currently favored by your constituents. Be simple. Ask for advice. Careful questions will uncover your competitor's weakness.

I-24

Wear out your competition with unrelenting attention to the needs of your constituents.

I-25

Where your competitor sees only one way to meet a need, discover two or three more. Divide the market

into smaller, more profitable segments. Think hard
about how you can benefit those you serve!

I-26
Learn more about the people who use your products.
Get better information. Create new products and services that fill previously unrecognized needs. Move
quickly before your competitor finds out.

I-27
These are the executive's keys to superiority. Use them
in the appropriate situations.

I-28
The executive who plans carefully in his office before
entering the competition understands how to leverage
his own strengths and those of his organization. With
careful plans, one can predict which alternatives for
action offer greater opportunities. With superior execution, one can turn these greater opportunities into ultimate victory.

WAGING WAR

Sun Tzu said:

In order to establish an army, the general needs thousands of chariots, tens of thousands of wagons and carts, and hundreds of thousands of soldiers. Supplies must be transported over thousands of *li*. There will be expenses for officers and staff, expenses for soldiers, expenses for chariots, leather armor, arrows, spears and swords, expenses for many different things. Thousands of *liang* (pieces) of gold will be expended each day to establish the army.

II
Competitive Actions

II-1

Competitive actions must be supported with personal and organization resources. The most important of these resources are your creativity and the commitment of your employees.

II-2

The greater the scope of the actions, the greater the expenditure of resources. Resources should be available before action is undertaken.

II-3

Quick victory is the aim of competitive action. If victory is delayed, then vision becomes dim and enthusiasm drains away. If a struggle is continued for a long time without results, the strength of people's determination will be exhausted.

II-4

When competitive actions are prolonged, resources will not be sufficient.

II-5

When your creativity is dulled, your commitment dampened, your enthusiasm drained, and your financing depleted, competitors will take advantage of your weakness. When that happens, no executive, however wise, can prevent the decline of his career and loss of business.

II-6

While we know that hastily executed competitive operations can be troublesome, we have never seen successful competitive operations that wasted time. A successful competitive operation need not be complicated. To win, do simple things well . . . and quickly!

II-7

Strategies that waste time and exhaust resources never work.

II-8

Executives who cannot balance risk with opportunity cannot profit in today's business environment. Speed and innovation are the keys. Only those who are comfortable with the pitfalls and ambiguities of rapid execution can profitably manage new products and services. Only those who appreciate the knowledge gained from quick failure can achieve lasting success.

II-9

A skillful executive does not hesitate to utilize the resources at his command. He engages the competition immediately. He gains precious information from direct contact with his constituents. He does not waste time talking to corporate staff people who are farther removed from the competitive situation than he is. Being one step ahead of the competition is worth more than anything else. Gaining that step is the wise executive's greatest desire.

II-10

A skillful executive builds the strongest possible team from the people in his company. He lets the competition show him how to serve better. In this way he is always increasing his constituent share. He builds his fortune through outstanding performance.

II-11

When an executive fails in competitive operations, it is due to overdependence on internal knowledge or folk wisdom. Folk wisdom is that body of unchallenged assumptions which everyone thinks to be true. Folk wisdom exists in every organization. The value of information offered by people who do not know constituents personally is almost zero, particularly in times of rapid change. Decisions made far from the constituents impoverish the executive.

II-12

Timely, accurate information is the lifeblood of successful competition. When obtained from outside sources, information is expensive. Expensive information wastes the company's resources.

II-13

The most expensive information is that which is out-of-date. Seventy percent of the value of information is gained from timeliness. Resources spent to gather yesterday's data are wasted. Maintaining yesterday's data consumes large portions of available money and manpower.

II-14

The wise executive harvests timely information from his constituents and his competitors. One new product idea generated from discussion with a real customer is worth any number of ideas generated by consultants or headquarters staff.

II-15

In order to dominate, you and your people—from top to bottom—must be passionate about the services you provide and the products you represent.

II-16

To capture the spirits of your employees, you must give them clearly defined and valuable rewards. You should reward the group for gaining customer share. But people should also be able to get rewards based on individual merit.

II-17

When someone provides outstanding service to a customer, reward him openly. Make his service an example for others to follow by providing sure and meaningful rewards for excellence.

II-18

Treat your employees well; train them thoroughly. The success of the organization is built on the individual success of its members.

II-19

This is how you can dominate one situation and create the resources to seize the next opportunity.

II-20

The important thing in competitive operations is quick results, not prolonged activity. The executive who understands how to excite his people and dominate a marketplace will become the foundation for his company.

MILITARY STRATEGY

Sun Tzu said:
In general, the best method for using the military force is to conquer an entire country; to destroy the country is inferior. Ancient warriors who knew how to use the military well defeated the enemy's army, but not by battle. They overpowered the enemy's country, but not by force. The goal was to take things whole. In this way, soldiers were not killed and our lord gained the largest booty. Therefore, a general who wins all his battles by destroying other armies is not the ultimate warrior. The ultimate warrior is one who wins the war by forcing the enemy to surrender without fighting any battles.

The best military strategy, then, is to use superior positioning. After that, use diplomacy. After that, use military force as a threat. Only after all else has failed, attack your enemy.

I I I
Competitive Strategy

III-1
It is generally better to dominate a whole organization or market with superior service and innovation than to splinter it with destructive tactics. To ruin a competitor is inferior to acquiring his resources intact.

III-2
To capture a competitor's constituency is better than to destroy his reputation; to recruit his productive employees is better than to destroy their jobs; to capture his distribution channels is better than tarnishing his company's image.

III-3
To win one hundred head-to-head battles with a competitor does not require great skill. To win the approval of an entire constituency without competitive battles (i.e., become a "sole source" provider of a service) is the ultimate goal. Those who reach this goal do so with a strategy of unrelenting attention to service. Instead of

fighting expensive head-to-head battles, they innovate to create superior products.

III-4
The ideal strategy is to make a competitor's products or services obsolete through innovation.

III-5
The next best strategy is to create better ways of providing products or services.

III-6
The next best strategy is to market yourself more effectively.

III-7
The worst strategy is to attack a competitor's reputation or product directly. This sort of strategy is a matter of desperation. It often results in the ruin of all parties involved.

III-8
To engage in destructive competition is ultimately self-defeating. Your aim is to provide superior service which generates high opinions among constituents. How can you do this by ruining competitors' reputations and perhaps destroying your own in the process?

III-9
If an executive is unable to control his impatience and seeks to destroy his competitors by direct attacks, he will waste at least one-third of his resources without

accomplishing much. The impact of such a strategy is disastrous.

III-10
The skillful executive conquers with knowledge and imagination. He creates better products; he uncovers unmet needs; he provides greater satisfaction. He out-flanks his competitors in the constituent's mind without resorting to head-to-head battles or lengthy campaigns.

III-11
Your aim is to take over a group of constituents intact by appearing superior in their minds. Thus, your resources will be preserved and your profit will be greater. This is the art of effective competitive strategy.

III-12
The philosophy of competitive strategy is this: If your customer base is already five to ten times larger than your competitors', press the competition hard through aggressive service. Dominate the situation with your presence. Spend your resources on research and inno-vation.

III-13
If you have twice as many customers, make sure you understand why they are choosing your product and why they might choose your competitors'. Talk with your constituents. Talk with your competitors' con-stituents. Redefine and differentiate yourself. How are you different? How are you superior?

III-14

If you share power and influence equally with your competitors, seek to divide the constituent group into smaller, more profitable niches which you can dominate. Further, seek new constituents for existing services. What additional services can you provide? Can you meet needs outside your currently defined constituency? Look at yourself through new eyes.

III-15

If you are weaker than your competition in a given situation, hold your position if you can, but be prepared to leave in favor of a more profitable constituency that you can dominate. Remember, many advantages flow from dominance. Greater profit is one; better morale is another. If an existing constituency is bleeding your resources, find or create another as fast as you can! A slow death is death nonetheless.

III-16

And if your products are in all respects inferior to your competitors', abandon those constituents. Even strong desire and intense effort cannot overcome fatal flaws. Invest your resources in a more promising situation.

III-17

Executives are leaders charged with the survival and growth of themselves and their organization. If a leader is smart and courageous, he and his organization will surely prosper and grow. If a leader is passive and weak, he and his organization will just as surely die. Success or failure is determined by leadership alone!

III-18
A high-ranking executive can cause trouble for himself and his organization in three ways:

III-19
First, he can cause trouble by acting out of ignorance. For instance, when ignorant that he should not begin competitive actions, he creates problems when he starts them anyway. Or, when ignorant that he is actually winning in ongoing competitive actions, he loses opportunity when he orders them stopped. High-ranking executives who issue orders without first-hand knowledge hobble themselves.

III-20
Second, he can cause trouble by focusing on rules rather than customers. When procedure-minded executives attempt to govern company actions with cumbersome rules, employees are confused and customer service suffers. Organizations whose purpose is to provide service for their own sake rather than for the sake of the customer (e.g., the federal government) can afford burdensome rules since customer service is not a priority. Aggressiveness, flexibility, and creativity, however, govern innovation and growth. An effective executive must thrive on uncertainty and ambiguity.

III-21
Third, he can cause trouble by promoting those without skill and courage. When an executive is appointed to a position of authority based on factors unrelated to ability, employees become skeptical and suspicious. This

inevitably lowers employee morale. Good leadership is everything! Authority must reside in the hands of those who can lead.

III-22
If employees are confused and demotivated by the actions of a high-ranking executive, competitors will steal away constituents. Internal weakness gives strength to competitors.

III-23
Five indicators predict who will dominate:

III-24
A leader who knows when to fight and when to retreat will win.

III-25
A leader who uses resources appropriate to the challenge at hand will win.

III-26
A leader who is enthusiastic and innovative will win.

III-27
A leader who uses accurate, timely information to make decisions will win.

III-28
A leader who is not burdened by onerous rules or troublesome staff will win.

III-29

If you know your constituents, your competitors, and yourself, your strategies will not fail, even if you are challenged a hundred times.

III-30

If you know yourself only, but are ignorant of your constituents or your competitors, you can expect to fail as often as you succeed.

III-31

If you are ignorant of yourself, in addition to your constituents and competitors, you will fail every time.

STRATEGIC DISPOSITIONS

Sun Tzu said:
Ancient great warriors first made themselves invincible. Then, they awaited the enemy's moment of vulnerability. Not to be conquered depends upon oneself; to conquer depends on the actions of the enemy. Thus, a skilled warrior can always remain unvanquished, but the enemy may not be vulnerable. Therefore, one who cannot conquer, defends. But one who can conquer, attacks.

Ancient warriors were not victorious through infinite wisdom or through boundless courage. Rather, ancient warriors made no mistakes. Every strategy foretold victory. Thus, those who defended well hid in the deepest recesses of the ninefold earth. Those who attacked well struck from the highest reaches of heaven. By waiting for the enemy's vulnerability, they surely triumphed.

IV
Positioning

IV-1

Effective executives position themselves and their products in situations where they will survive. Then they wait for an opportunity to act.

IV-2

Survival depends on one's own actions; the opportunity to triumph depends on the actions of others.

IV-3

Therefore, while an effective executive can always manage to survive, he may not necessarily be able to triumph.

IV-4

It is said: The way to win may be known, but victory itself cannot be forced.

IV-5

Survival depends on a careful defense; victory results from taking the initiative and acting at the right moment.

Sun Tzu said:
A great general establishes his position where he cannot be defeated. He misses no opportunity to exploit the weakness of his enemy. A winning general creates the conditions of victory before beginning the war. A losing general begins the war before knowing how to win it. A great commander first cultivates his own character and develops a strong organization. In this way, he effectively manages those factors which are crucial to his success or failure.

The elements of strategy are first, measuring; second, estimating; third, calculating; fourth, comparing; and fifth, victory. The terrain creates measurements. Estimates are based on measurements. Calculations on estimates. Comparisons on calculations. And, victory on comparisons. Thus, a victorious army fights its opponents like a heavy weight against a light weight, or like a large river rushing through a narrow gorge. It cannot be stopped. Success in war is a matter of positioning.

IV-6

If your resources are not adequate, use a defensive approach. When the time is right, move quickly.

IV-7

Effective executives defend positions that cannot be attacked. Effective executives initiate actions from positions of supreme advantage. Thus, they achieve victory without the risk of being defeated.

IV-8

To control a situation through confrontation or emotion does not indicate superior ability. After all, it takes no great skill to embarrass others into retreat.

IV-9

Neither does winning a heated argument in a public place.

IV-10

Highly effective executives win victories which seem easy.

IV-11

Highly effective executives are not people of extraordinary wisdom or reckless courage.

IV-12

Rather, highly effective executives win because they make no mistakes. Because they are competent, every strategy they employ contributes to their eventual triumph. By waiting for others to provide the opportunity, they position themselves to win.

IV-13

Effective executives establish positions where they can survive. They miss no chance to exploit opportunities provided by their constituents.

IV-14

A winning executive creates the conditions of victory before taking any initiative. A losing executive takes initiative before knowing how to succeed.

IV-15

Once in a strong position, an effective executive cultivates his own character and develops a responsive organization. In this way, he controls those factors that are crucial to his success or failure.

IV-16

In taking the initiative, he carefully considers strategy. The elements of strategy are: identifying opportunity; gathering facts; analyzing alternatives; judging appropriateness; and taking action.

IV-17

The situation, i.e., the actions or decisions of others in the market or in the organization, creates opportunity.

IV-18

Facts clarify the situation. Alternatives are based on the facts. Appropriateness is based on evaluation of alternatives. And action is based on appropriateness.

IV-19

An effective executive dominates his constituents like a heavy weight against a light weight or a like a large river rushing through a narrow gorge. His momentum cannot be stopped.

IV-20

The ability to triumph is a matter of positioning. Wait for the opportunity created by others. Execute effective strategies at the appropriate time.

STRATEGIC POWER

Sun Tzu said:
Fighting many is the same as fighting few. It is a question of formations and communications. Any army can fight without losing. It is a question of the orthodox or the unorthodox. When an army overcomes the enemy like a millstone smashing eggs, it is a question of emptiness and fullness. The enemy does not know where to defend.

For a skilled commander, momentum is like a drawn crossbow and timing is the trigger which will release the bolt with deadly accuracy. So, a great warrior creates momentum; then, at the right moment, he hurls his troops at the enemy like rolling round rocks down the side of a mountain. His victory is a matter of momentum and timing.

V 兵
Opportunity and Timing

V-1

The principles used to lead a large group are the same as those used to lead a small group. It is a matter of appropriate organization.

V-2

Taking on a strong competitor is the same as taking on a weak competitor. It is a matter of creating favorable opportunities and using the power of timing.

V-3

Generally, an executive can survive within the power structure of his organization. It is a matter of taking appropriate actions and providing adequate service to his constituency.

V-4

But when an executive dominates a situation, it is because he creates opportunity and understands timing. It is a matter of showing strength and apparent weakness, reality and illusion. Competitors do not know what to defend against.

V-5

In competitive situations, expected tactics are normally used to confront the opponent. But it is the power created by the use of unexpected tactics—that is, innovative use of people and information—that makes victory certain.

V-6

The executive who is skillful at using unexpected tactics has infinite resources. For him, moving from expected tactics to unexpected tactics and back again flows smoothly like the surface of a great river.

V-7

The expected and the unexpected end and begin again, like the sun and the moon. They cycle from death to life, like the four seasons.

V-8

There are only five notes in music; but we could not in a lifetime hear their infinite combinations.

V-9

There are only five colors in painting; but we could not in a lifetime see their infinite combinations.

V-10

There are only five flavors in cooking; but we could not in a lifetime taste their infinite combinations.

V-11

Competition within organizations and in the marketplace gives rise to opportunities for both expected and unexpected tactics. We could not in a lifetime exhaust the possibilities provided by the innovative use of people and information.

V-12

Expected and unexpected tactics create one another in the ebb and flow of conflict, like a circle with no starting point. Your opponents cannot tell where one ends and the other begins.

V-13

When the force of rushing water pushes huge boulders out of the way, it is due to overwhelming power.

V-14

When the speed of a diving falcon breaks the neck of its prey, it is due to precise timing.

V-15

For the skilled executive, opportunity is like a launching pad and timing is the trigger that will shoot a missile with deadly accuracy.

V-16

The skilled executive creates a situation of intense pressure for his competitor and times his actions with unfailing results.

V-17

In the chaos of organizational politics or the competitive marketplace, the skilled executive recognizes patterns in the activities of his rivals, while he seems to be using his resources randomly, almost moving in circles. He appears confused, but he cannot be defeated.

V-18

Apparent disorder comes from expert organization. The illusion of fear comes from great courage. Seeming weakness comes from realized strength.

V-19

A highly effective executive, skillful at maneuvering competitors in competitive situations, creates favorable opportunities by luring his competitors into vulnerable positions with the promise of easy gain. There he waits with the overwhelming power derived from combining the expected with the unexpected, the obvious with the innovative.

V-20

In this way, the wise executive creates victory with his own initiative. He does not depend on others to give him success.

V-21

He selects the most appropriate people to carry out his purposes at the critical moment.

V-22
The people he uses must be like round stones. Any stone, regardless of shape, is peaceful when resting on a level place. When the ground is uneven, and force is applied, a round stone will move easily.

V-23
So, a skillful executive creates uneven circumstances that operate in his favor; then, at the right moment, he hurls his chosen people at his competitor as if he were rolling round stones down the side of a steep mountain.

EMPTINESS AND FULLNESS

Sun Tzu said:
A skillful warrior moves his opponent; he does not allow the opponent to move him. Against a skilled attacker, the enemy does not know which point to defend; against a skilled defender, the enemy does not know which point to attack. Formless and invisible, we are the arbiter of the enemy's fate. One is strong if he causes the enemy to respond to him; one is weak if one must respond to the enemy.

Therefore, the great general entraps the enemy but retains his own freedom. He creates overwhelming advantage where the enemy is weak. According to my way of thinking, even if the opponent has a larger number of soldiers, how can this help him win if I control the situation?

VI
Control

VI-1
Those who prepare quickly and thoroughly await the
encounter at ease; those who prepare later are rushed
and exhausted.

VI-2
A skillful executive moves his competition; he does not
allow the competition to move him.

VI-3
A skillful executive lures his competitor to advance by
offering him apparent advantages; he prevents his competitor from attacking by revealing apparent disadvantages.
Hence, his competition advances only when he is ready.

VI-4
He keeps his rivals on the move and in the dark. If a competitor is comfortable, he creates difficulty. If a competitor is satisfied, he creates dissatisfaction. If a
competitor is calm, he creates agitation.

VI-5

The skilled executive appears where the competition must rush to defend against him; he goes where his competitors least expect to find him.

VI-6

A skillful executive positions his resources with ease because he begins by occupying territory not contested by others.

VI-7

A superbly effective executive's offensive moves always succeed because he attacks points that cannot be defended. A superbly effective executive's defensive positions never fail because he defends points that cannot be attacked.

VI-8

Against such a skilled attacker, the competition does not know which points to defend; against such a skilled defender, the competition does not know which points to attack.

VI-9

The best strategies are subtle. They have no discernible form. The best strategies are hidden. They cannot be discovered. Formless and invisible, one can control a competitor's destiny.

VI-10

When a skilled executive pressures his competition, he focuses on weak points and cannot be stopped. When a skilled executive changes his position, he moves swiftly and cannot be knocked off his course.

VI-11
If all considerations indicate that it is time for an encounter, even when a competitor hides behind a large reputation or a closed door, he must emerge if an important issue or a critical market is threatened.

VI-12
If it is time for an encounter, even if a competitor postures and threatens, he can do no harm if no target is available for him to aim at.

VI-13
A superbly effective executive moves the competition but retains his own freedom. He divides the competition while he keeps himself intact. He distracts the competition while he remains focused. Hence, he is able to use many resources to pressure points that are supported with fewer resources. He creates overwhelming leverage. He concentrates strength against weakness.

VI-14
The less a competitor knows about where we intend to focus our attention, the stronger we are. If the competitor must spread his resources to too many places to meet our challenge, each place will be weaker.

VI-15
If a competitor strengthens one department, he weakens another. If he strengthens one product, he weakens

Sun Tzu said:

Victory can be crafted. Even if the enemy is numerous, I can make him lose his will to fight. Therefore, I probe carefully to determine which strategies can win and which will lose. I spar with the enemy to determine what he will defend and when he will attack. I assume various positions to determine where he is strong and where he is weak. I compare my army with his to determine relative sufficiency and insufficiency. When I develop my final strategy, I make sure it is formless and invisible. A formless strategy cannot be discovered by the best spy; an invisible strategy cannot be defeated by the wisest counselors. I defeat the enemy by controlling the situation, but the enemy does not know how I control it. Even though all can see afterwards how a victory was accomplished, none can understand the reasoning which led to the development of a specific strategy.

another. If he concentrates on one constituency, he ignores others. If he tries to be strong everywhere, he will be weak everywhere.

VI-16
One is strong if he causes the competition to react to him; one is weak if he must react to the competition.

VI-17
If an executive controls the time and place of an encounter, he can make careful, detailed preparations without risking failure. If one does not control the time and place of battle, no matter how many resources are thrown into the conflict, preparations will be inadequate and failure will occur.

VI-18
According to my way of thinking, if I control the situation, how can the competition's resources help them, even if they are greatly superior?

VI-19
So it is said: With control, victory can be crafted by those with skill. Even if a competitor's resources are mighty, with control, I can make him lose his will to fight.

VI-20
Therefore, I probe carefully to determine which strategies can win and which will lose.

VI-21

I spar with the competition to determine what points they will defend and where they intend to attack.

VI-22

I assume various positions to determine where they are strong and where they are weak.

VI-23

I compare my resources with their resources to determine relative sufficiency and insufficiency.

VI-24

When I develop my final strategy, I make sure it is formless and invisible to my competitor. A formless strategy cannot be discovered by the best spy; an invisible strategy cannot be defeated by the sharpest consultants.

VI-25

I defeat the competition by controlling the situation, but my competitors cannot discover how I control it. Even though all can see that victory was accomplished, none can understand how I actually did it. My results are obvious, my methods are hidden.

VI-26

Successful strategies should never be repeated. Each conflict represents a unique situation.

VI-27

Successful strategies flow like water; they are shaped by the circumstances of the conflict. When water flows, it avoids the high ground and seeks the low ground. Successful strategies likewise avoid difficult methods and find easy ones.

VI-28

Just as the flow of water is shaped by the contour of the land, the flow of victory is shaped by the actions of the opponent.

VI-29

As water has no constant form, the tactics of victory have no constant form.

VI-30

In nature, no single element is superior to all others in every situation. Each of the four seasons comes and goes. Some days are longer and some days are shorter. The moon waxes and wanes.

VI-31

Thus, the executive who crafts his victory by successfully adapting his plans and resources to the strengths and weakness of his opponent is called a genius.

MANEUVERING THE ARMY

Sun Tzu said:
Nothing is more difficult than maneuvering the army. Maneuvering successfully depends on misdirecting the enemy and luring them away. In this way, even if you start later than the enemy, you will arrive on the battlefield first. Move toward situations of advantage. Retain your freedom. He who moves without restriction will win. Ancient warriors won by deception. The secret of deception is knowing how to manipulate the enemy's perceptions. Make the far seem near and the near seem far. Make the direct seem indirect and the indirect seem direct.

VII
Managing Direct Conflict

VII-1
Once an executive understands the need to take on a competitor, he gathers his resources, organizes them carefully, and brings them under his control.

VII-2
The most difficult aspect of competition on any level is direct attack on a competitor. Winning in a direct attack depends on using information effectively. In planning an attack, gather information from the competitor and from the marketplace. Determine where the real advantages and disadvantages lie. Determine what is real and what is illusion.

VII-3
Further, control the information you give your competitor. By controlling information well, you can misdirect the competitor and lead him astray. You can make him adopt a less effective strategy by creating false perceptions. Thus, even if you start out later than your competitor, you can arrive first. Only those who understand the subtleties of controlling information can achieve this.

VII-4

Direct attack can be used to gain an advantage; or, direct attack can be used to avoid a loss.

VII-5

If you seek to gain an advantage, timing is critical. Do not mobilize unnecessary resources before you advance. This will slow you down. Your competitor will escape and whatever opportunity you had will be lost.

VII-6

On the other hand, do not fragment your resources in order to advance in the name of speed.

VII-7

If you skip over necessary preparation and move hastily into a difficult conflict situation, even if you work day and night, you will have little chance of success. Your efforts will be scattered. Your resources wasted. Your motivation destroyed.

VII-8

Adequate preparation—determining what mix of resources to apply at what time—is essential to succeed in direct attack. It is unwise to risk anything less.

VII-9

If you lack effective training or proper equipment, you will be defeated. If you lack adequate financial backing, you will be defeated. If you lack timely information, you will be defeated.

VII-10

The executive who does not know his competitor's objectives, resources, and allies cannot know with whom to form alliances. If he does not know the minds of constituents and the political and market environment, he cannot focus his resources.

VII-11

If an executive does not employ inside informants and consultants to discover his opponent's strengths and weaknesses, he cannot make successful plans.

VII-12

Succeeding in a direct attack on a competitor depends on deceiving him. If your stratagems are known to your competitor, no matter how good they are, he can defeat them. Focus on your objective, and keep your strategy secret. By constantly changing form, keep your competitor off balance.

VII-13

In this way, your methods are hidden. You can move as swiftly as a gale or as slowly as a breeze. You can attack like fierce fire. You can stand like an unshaken mountain. You can strike like lightning, powerful and unpredictable from the darkness.

VII-14

Divide the competition's manpower and you will be able to plunder his constituency. Cause him to lose his focus and you will conquer.

Sun Tzu said:

A good general avoids the enemy when his spirits are high. He attacks when the enemy is tired. A good general waits for chaos with order. A good general waits for the enemy to come from a distance. Do not attack a well-ordered formation. Do not advance up a hill. Do not retreat down a slope. Do not pursue a false retreat. Do not attack crack troops. Do not take the enemy's bait. Do not intercept an enemy who is returning home. When you surround an enemy, give him a way out. Do not press a desperate enemy. This is the essence of maneuvering an army.

VII-15

If you move without restriction, while hampering the movements of your competitors, you will win.

VII-16

The secret of winning a direct attack is knowing how to manipulate perceptions. Make distant threats seem near and nearby threats seem distant. Make unworkable strategies seem productive and workable strategies seem unproductive.

VII-17

Direct attacks generate emotion. In circumstances where emotions are high, wise reasoning may be hindered. Further, clear communication among members of your group can be more difficult.

VII-18

For this reason, develop certain devices which can be used to refocus attention—both your own and that of your employees—on your objectives. If your employees are unified by clear communication, those who are aggressive will not attempt unwise initiatives and those who are overly cautious will not ignore opportunities for gain. This is the way people are managed during conflict.

VII-19

Remember, however, that your emotions and communicating signals will also be read by your competitor. Therefore, confuse your competitor by mixing false signals with real ones. But, fooling a competitor requires a high level of self-discipline and commitment among members of your group.

VII-20
The competition's manpower can be demotivated; a hostile executive can be distracted from his purpose.

VII-21
If you watch a competitor closely, you will observe that his spirit is high in the early stages. Later, his spirit will diminish. As matters drag on, he will be anxious for a resolution. Use this to your advantage.

VII-22
Avoid the competitor when his spirits are high. Pressure him when he is lazy or tired. Time your actions according to the spirit of the competitor.

VII-23
Await a chaotic competitor with discipline. Await a disordered competitor with calm. In this way, you control your emotions.

VII-24
Wait for the competition to come to you. Gather critical information. Analyze it in depth. In this way, you and your group will be thoroughly prepared.

VII-25
Do not force an encounter with a well-prepared competitor in haste. Do not challenge a well-managed group quickly. Wait for the situation to change.

VII-26
Manage a direct conflict in this way. Do not challenge

strong, easily defended products or issues. Do not retreat into a position of weakness.

VII-27
Do not pursue the competitor when he appears to move away from a strong market or issue. This may be a false retreat to lure you away also.

VII-28
Do not attack the competitor's sharpest people.

VII-29
Do not grab an apparent advantage without investigation. It may be bait in a competitor's trap.

VII-30
If your competitor is withdrawing from your marketplace, do not chase him. He is already defeated.

VII-31
When a competitor has exhausted his resources, give him a way out. Let him retain his ability to earn a living. Do not attempt to destroy him. This may prove to be a costly way to win.

VII-32
There is no need to press a desperate competitor. Desperation itself will bring defeat.

VII-33
This is the essence of winning in direct attack.

THE NINE POSSIBILITIES

Sun Tzu said:

Only a general who is flexible and knows how to adapt his strategy to changing circumstances can command victorious troops. Therefore, do not garrison troops in abandoned lands. Unite with allies where roads intersect. Do not linger in desperate ground. Make contingency plans in surrounded land. Fight if attacked in dead lands. Do not assume the enemy will not come. Prepare for his coming. Do not assume the enemy will not attack. Rely instead on a strong defense.

VIII
Flexibility

VIII-1

Once an executive has decided to enter into competition for a group of constituents, he should follow these rules.

VIII-2

Do not set up a position that is isolated or far from resources.

VIII-3

Do not set up a position that has many weak points and cannot be defended.

VIII-4

Communicate with allies and arrange for mutual support.

VIII-5

Make contingency plans in case the competition moves quickly to challenge your position.

VIII-6
If pressed into action, be ready to delay an encounter until you are ready.

VIII-7
In making strategic choices, some methods should not be used; some people should not be attacked; some issues should not be argued; and some markets should not be contested.

VIII-8
In the midst of competition, sometimes communications from distant staff members should not be acknowledged.

VIII-9
Therefore, only an executive who is flexible and can adapt his strategy to changes in circumstances can effectively manage his resources in competition.

VIII-10
An executive who is not flexible enough to adapt his strategy to changes in circumstances, even if he has wide knowledge of people and methods, will not take advantage of this knowledge.

VIII-11
An executive who is not flexible enough to adapt his strategy to changes in circumstances, even if he can recognize advantageous situations, will not assign the right person to do the right things at the right time.

VIII-12

A wise executive considers both gains and losses in his strategic calculations.

VIII-13

By considering gains, his plans can be trusted to yield the maximum profit; by considering losses, he can foresee problems and modify his plans to overcome them.

VIII-14

A wise executive creates losses for the competition to constrain him from movement.

VIII-15

He uses minor irritations to keep his competitor occupied. He uses superficial benefits to move him about and keep him busy.

VIII-16

So, to be effective in competition, do not assume your competitor will not attack; instead rely on preparation to assure your victory and on strong defenses to defeat him.

VIII-17

There are five character flaws that we can use to defeat an executive engaged in competition.

VIII-18

If he is reckless, we can cause him to waste his resources.

Sun Tzu said:

There are five character flaws which are dangerous for a general: If he is reckless, his men can be killed. If he is cowardly, his army can be captured. If he is short-tempered, he will react in anger. If he is self-important, he can be deceived. If he is attached to his men, he will hesitate at a critical moment. These five flaws are certainly unfortunate for the general, but they cause great destruction in war. These five flaws cause generals to fail and armies to die. Consider them well.

VIII-19

If he is timid, we can usurp his resources.

VIII-20

If he is short-tempered, we can cause him to be rash.

VIII-21

If he is self-important, we can deceive him by flattery.

VIII-22

If he is overly concerned about his popularity, he will hesitate before making an unpopular decision at a critical moment.

VIII-23

These five flaws greatly restrict an executive's potential success. They cause tremendous loss in competitive situations.

VIII-24

These five flaws cause executives to fail and companies to die. Eliminate them in yourself.

Deploying Troops

Sun Tzu said:

Use the following rules. Cross the mountains by following the valleys. Stay on the high ground where you have a clear view of the surrounding country. Do not face uphill to fight. When the enemy is crossing water, it is advantageous to attack when half of his troops have crossed over. When crossing a swamp, move quickly. Keep away from gorges, hollows, and crevices which form natural traps and snares. If the enemy's troops must lean on their weapons in order to stand upright, they are hungry. If the enemy's water carriers drink first, the entire enemy troop is thirsty. If enemy troops clamor during the night, the enemy is fearful. When the enemy feeds his war horses grain and kills his pack horses for meat, when the enemy's soldiers do not hang up their cooking pots nor return to their shelters, the enemy is desperate.

IX
Maneuvering

IX-1
When the time has come to meet the competition, use the following rules. Move around obstacles and difficulties, rather than through them. Gather together the most knowledgeable people, organize them appropriately, train them effectively, and equip them well.

IX-2
Do not tackle difficult problems with inadequate resources.

IX-3
If you must reorganize your group before an encounter, do so quickly. Move toward a stable organization. When the competition is reorganizing, do not challenge him when he begins because he will revert to his former structure in order to meet you. It is more advantageous to wait until reorganization is halfway complete and all is in chaos.

IX-4

If you are in the midst of intense competition, do not institute large-scale organizational change yourself. Stick with acceptable, easily understood methods and procedures. Maintain stable organization patterns.

IX-5

Keep administrative matters simple and clear. Do not waste time with unnecessary paperwork.

IX-6

You can manage competition more easily when your emotions, your organization, and your constituency are stable.

IX-7

Different competitive situations may require different tactics for success. But, as far as possible, maintain stability during conflict situations. Do things the easy, well-understood way. Operate from positions which can be defended.

IX-8

Most groups like stability. People work better with methods, procedures, and equipment they understand. They are more comfortable if they know what is going on. They dislike being in the dark. People who are comfortable and stable have healthier emotions and sharper minds. Healthy emotions and sharp minds are necessary for competitive success.

IX-9

When you face a challenge or obstacle, focus on the benefits of success. Create motivation through enthusiasm.

IX-10

In this way, your group draws strength from your example.

IX-11

When there is excessive change or uncertainty in the situation, it will affect your ability to compete. If you must work within a rapidly changing or highly uncertain situation, wait until the flood of change or uncertainty has subsided. There are also dangers inherent in every competitive situation because of commonly held assumptions or assertions of undocumented facts. I call this "folk wisdom." Challenge the validity of folk wisdom.

IX-12

Stay away from folk wisdom. If your competitor bases his movements on it, push him as far as possible in the direction he is going. Most folk wisdom cannot be proven, so an opponent who bases his defense on it is greatly weakened.

IX-13

When you must compete in an environment that allows only incomplete understanding of the movements or tactics of the competition, be particularly careful to search for traps or ambushes. Challenge anything which appears unusual.

IX-14

If your competitor is ready to challenge but remains calm, it is likely that he has some crucial advantage to rely on. Look for it. If your competitor seems unprepared for conflict, but he challenges you from afar, he wants you to leave your defensive positions and advance. This is because he occupies a position which gives him an advantage. Investigate it thoroughly.

IX-15

If there is unexplained activity in the market or agitation among members of your constituency, your competition may be moving behind a screen.

IX-16

When your competitor sets hidden traps and obstacles, he is trying to confuse you. If ordinarily supportive constituents suddenly distance themselves from you, your competitor is preparing to make a sudden attack.

IX-17

Watch for signs from your competitor's group. If there is a great deal of erratic activity, he may be preparing to move quickly. If the activity level is steady and organized, he is preparing to move cautiously. Look for patterns of activity that show where he is gathering information.

IX-18

If your competitor's communications sound self-effacing, but he appears confident, he is preparing to advance.

IX-19
If your competitor's communications are evasive ,
aggressive in tone, he is preparing to withdraw.

IX-20
If your competitor comes to you with a generous offer
to consider, he may need time to rest.

IX-21
If your competitor, without any apparent reason, suddenly wants to begin peace negotiations, then he is plotting.

IX-22
If your competitor deploys his resources in an aggressive manner, he is expecting an encounter.

IX-23
If your competitor partially advances and then partially
retreats, he is trying to lure you out of your defensive
position.

IX-24
If your competitor must use trickery or subterfuge to
sustain his position, he is facing some kind of shortage.

IX-25
If your competitor sees an obvious advantage, but fails
to advance, he is tired.

IX-26
If your competitor wanders aimlessly in discussion, he
is uncertain.

Sun Tzu said:

In war we do not need to have the largest army in order to win. It is important not to advance recklessly. When we concentrate our forces so they match those of the enemy, if we respect the enemy's strength and carefully study his movements, we will win. If we underestimate the enemy and do not consider the meaning of his movements, we will lose.

IX-27
If your competitor speaks loudly, he is afraid.

IX-28
If your competitor's group is in turmoil, his leadership is not effective.

IX-29
If your competitor's communications are in disarray, his thinking is chaotic.

IX-30
If your competitor's representatives are short-tempered, they are under emotional stress.

IX-31
When your competitor uses his last available resources to challenge you, he is desperate.

IX-32
When your competitor's people whisper among themselves in clandestine groups, your competitor is losing their loyalty.

IX-33
When your competitor hands out too many rewards, he has lost the ability to motivate his group. When your competitor hands out too many punishments, he has lost control of his people.

IX-34
When your competitor publicly criticizes his constituency, he is not very smart.

IX-35
When a competitor confronts you as if prepared for an encounter, but neither advances nor retreats, you must study the situation carefully. Search for important factors you may have overlooked.

IX-36
In conflict we do not necessarily need to have the most resources to win. It is important, however, that we do not challenge others recklessly.

IX-37
If you concentrate your resources, respect a competitor's strength, and carefully study his movements, you will win. If you underestimate a competitor's strength and do not consider the meaning of his movements, you will lose.

IX-38
When managing people, if you criticize an individual before he feels loyalty to you, he will not obey your orders in the future. Further, after a person feels loyalty, if discipline is not enforced, he will not follow orders either. Without obedience, it is hard to use people effectively.

IX-39
Therefore, if you direct your employees through an appropriate organization structure and maintain control through appropriate discipline, your people will be competent.

IX-40

If you train and organize your employees with clear
expectations, they can be relied on in a competitive situation. If you train and organize your group with vague
expectations, they cannot be relied on.

IX-41

When expectations are clear and organization structure
is appropriate for the task, people will trust their leaders.

Terrain

Sun Tzu said:
We describe terrain as accessible, ensnaring, suspending, narrow, mountainous, and remote. If the forces of both sides can enter and leave the battlefield without difficulty, then the battlefield is accessible. If it is easy for our forces to enter the battlefield, but difficult to withdraw, then the battlefield is entrapping. If the forces of both sides have difficulty entering and leaving the battlefield, then the battlefield is suspending. Narrow battlefields have restricted access routes, such as through constricted passes or deep valleys. On a mountainous battlefield, if our forces arrive first, take the high ground. Remote battlefields are equally risky for both sides.

X 兵

Types of Competitive Situations and Causes of Failure

X-1
We can describe the six competitive situations as accessible, ensnaring, inconclusive, restricted, difficult, and speculative.

X-2
If all competitors can reach a given constituency easily, then the situation is accessible. When the situation is accessible, try to establish a strong position first. This gives you an advantageous position.

X-3
If it is easy for either side to enter into a competitive situation, but once involved, difficult to withdraw, then the situation is ensnaring. When your competitor is unprepared, you can challenge him. However, remember that once you are involved, if your investment in

Sun Tzu said:

During a campaign, disaster can spring from six different mistakes of the commanding general. The mistakes are desertion, insubordination, ineffectiveness, rashness, chaos, and incompetence.

Those who are experienced at war advance only when they have knowledge; as a result, they have no need to retreat. Thus it is said: Know the enemy and know yourself, you will not lose; know the seasons and know the battlefield, too, then your victory will be complete.

money or manpower is high, you may not be able to withdraw. Therefore, it is disadvantageous to challenge your competitor if he is prepared.

X-4

If both sides have difficulty entering and leaving a competitive situation, then neither side may be able to win. Do not challenge a competitor when you are not confident of winning, even if he is weak. It is a waste of resources. Instead, if you can, make your competitor waste *his* resources. Wait for a better moment for an encounter.

X-5

Restricted markets are difficult to access. Stringent technological requirements, professional knowledge, or financial demands may present significant challenges. If you are able to access the constituency *first,* build even stronger barriers. From this position, you have the advantage and you can afford to wait for your competitor's advance. If your competitor has already established himself in this market strongly, he has the advantage. Do not attack unless he has left you an opening.

X-6

Where both sides have difficulty accessing a constituency, if you arrive first, set up strong defensive positions and wait for your competitor to advance. If your competitor already has a strong defensive position, make him waste time and money defending his territory. But, do not move too quickly if he begins to retreat. This may be a trap.

X-7

Speculative competitive situations involve important or profitable constituents who are unknown or remote. These situations are equally risky for both sides because they may involve taking actions whose costs and consequences are largely unclear. In a speculative situation, it is usually difficult to create circumstances in which we can win. Therefore it is generally not advantageous to advance.

X-8

These are the principles for six different types of competitive situations. When an executive begins to move resources toward an objective, he must carefully examine his campaign plans in light of these principles.

X-9

During competitive operations, failure can spring from six different conditions. These conditions are not created by fate, but are caused by executive mistakes. These conditions are lack of resources, lack of direction, lack of performance, lack of discipline, lack of order, and lack of competence.

X-10

If, all other things being equal, an executive orders a poorly equipped, supplied, trained, organized, or funded group to challenge another group that is adequate in these areas, the cause of the ensuing failure is lack of resources.

X-11
If the people in a group are strong-willed but their managers are weak, the cause of failure is lack of direction.

X-12
If a group's managers are strong-willed but the people are poorly trained or demotivated, the cause of failure is lack of performance.

X-13
When operating executives are angry or defiant, or when they become emotional and challenge competitors without receiving orders to do so, the cause of failure is lack of discipline.

X-14
When the chief executive is weak and lacks personal authority, when he cannot motivate people and training is poor, or when people's tasks are unclear and organization structure is vague, the cause of failure is lack of order.

X-15
When the chief executive cannot develop effective operating plans, when he misunderstands competitors' actions, or when he underestimates the resources needed to complete tasks, the cause of failure is lack of competence.

X-16
These six conditions lead to failure. Every executive needs to investigate them carefully and remove them from himself.

X-17

The competitive situation can be a great ally to an executive. An effective executive understands his constituents, his opponent, himself, and the realities all parties face, and thereby controls victory; he correctly estimates the difficulty of alternate strategies and calculates the resources required. He accurately assesses those factors that require his attention immediately and those which can be dealt with later. He knows the strengths, weaknesses, and capacity of the people involved in the situation—both his own and those loyal to his opponent. An effective executive wins because he takes the time to know all these things and applies his knowledge to take advantage of the opportunities he uncovers.

X-18

Therefore, if the chief executive calculates that success is probable, he should go ahead, even if his advisors think differently. If he calculates failure, he should stop, even if his advisors want to go ahead.

X-19

An executive who competes, but does not seek to gain personal glory; who acts, but does not seek to avoid responsibility; whose only goal is to benefit his constituents and his organization is the company's most precious asset.

X-20

Treat your associates like your own family and they will work for you. Treat them like your beloved friends and they will repay you with loyalty.

X-21

But, if you are so generous with your associates and employees that you cannot manage them, so kind you cannot maintain order or direct them when they are confused, it is like spoiling your children. Once spoiled, they are not effective.

X-22

In timing my actions, if I know my group has the resources to succeed, but I do not know whether my competitor is vulnerable, my chances of victory are half.

X-23

If I know my competitor is vulnerable, but I do not know if my group has the resources to succeed, my chances of victory are half.

X-24

If I know my competitor is vulnerable, and I know my group has the resources to succeed, but I do not know if the competitive situation allows me to win, my chances of victory are also half.

X-25

Hence, those executives who experience success advance only when they have knowledge; as a result, they have no need to retreat.

X-26

Know your opponent and know yourself, you will not lose; know the competitive situation and the constituents involved, also, then your success will be complete.

THE NINEFOLD EARTH

Sun Tzu said:
The battlefield situation determines whether it is
more advantageous to advance or to withdraw. In
a scattered situation, avoid a fight. In an uncommitted situation, keep the elements of the army in
close contact with each other. In a competitive situation, do not attack. In an accessible situation, do
not cease to be diligent. In an intersecting situation,
consolidate your alliances. In a critical situation,
seize important positions. In a surrounded situation, block access routes. In a deadly situation, tell
the army it may not survive.

XI
Competitive Conditions and Offensive Strategy

XI-1
Proper application of the principles of offensive strategy requires analysis of the competitive situation. The competitive situation determines whether it is more advantageous to advance or to withdraw. The competitive situation determines how we can effectively employ our resources. The different kinds of situations must be examined carefully.

XI-2
When a competitor attempts to challenge us before we can concentrate our resources, we are in a *scattered situation*.

XI-3
If we are advancing into our competitor's territory, but we have expended only a few resources, we are in an *uncommitted situation*.

XI-4

If we are trying to occupy a profitable position which is also profitable for our competitor to occupy, we are in a *conflict situation.*

XI-5

If we can advance and retreat easily, but it is also easy for the competition to advance and retreat, we are in an *accessible situation.*

XI-6

If the position we want overlaps several constituencies, and allows us to access the resources of the overlapped constituencies, we are in an *intersecting situation.*

XI-7

When we have penetrated deeply into another's territory and we have expended large amounts of resources, we are in a *critical situation.*

XI-8

When we must overcome technical, financial, or organizational challenges, or there are major barriers to reaching the constituents we want, we are in a *blocked situation.*

XI-9

When we have expended resources to obtain constituents and it is difficult to recover our investment, but easy for competitors to challenge our position, we are in a *surrounded situation.*

XI-10

When we can survive only if we challenge and win quickly, but we will perish if we delay, we are in a *deadly situation*.

XI-11

In a *scattered situation*, avoid a fight. Concentrate your resources to multiply their effect. In an *uncommitted situation*, keep resources focused on the goal.

XI-12

In a *conflict situation*, do not advance. Approach the competitor from his blind side; create some kind of advantage before expending resources. In an *accessible situation*, keep up your guard. Plan your defenses carefully.

XI-13

In an *intersecting situation*, consolidate your alliances. In a *critical situation*, take important positions first. Make sure your technical, financial, and organizational resources are adequate.

XI-14

In a *blocked situation*, overcome the challenges and barriers quickly. In a *surrounded situation*, hinder your competitor's ability to attack by blocking his access to your constituents. Execute a strategy for escaping the trap. In a *deadly situation*, face the fact that you may not survive. Advance quickly; expend your resources in trying to win. Do not accept a slow death.

Sun Tzu said:

The business of the commanding general is to bring all the forces together and put them into a dangerous situation. Lead troops by action, not by words. The troops of those skilled in leadership are like the "Simultaneously Responding" serpent. The "Simultaneously Responding" serpent lives in the mountains of Chang. If its head is threatened, its tail will swiftly attack. If its tail is threatened, its head will attack. If its body is threatened, both head and tail will attack at the same time. In the same way, the goal of leadership is to make the soldiers think and fight as one team.

XI-15

In managing competitive actions, effective executives make it difficult for competitors to defend all aspects of their positions. They make it difficult for competitors to coordinate use of resources. They make it difficult for competitors to support weaker organizational elements. They make it difficult for competitors to communicate with constituents.

XI-16

When a competitor's resources are spread around, effective executives prevent their concentration. When resources are concentrated, effective executives prevent their coordination.

XI-17

Effective executives advance their position when it is advantageous and stop when it is not.

XI-18

You may ask at this point: "How can I defeat a well-prepared, well-managed competitor who is about to confront me?" The answer is: "Get something the competitor wants. Then he will comply with your desires."

XI-19

Speed is the major factor in successful competitive action. You must take advantage of the situation before your competitor arrives. Exploit his lack of readiness. Attack his weakest spot.

XI-20

In general, competitive actions will succeed only if people are wholly committed to them. When people are committed, they have a unified purpose. When they are unified, no defender can overcome them. The nature of people is to ardently strive to reach a goal when they are committed. Put your organization into a situation where they have no choice but to commit to your goals, and they will succeed beyond their limits.

XI-21

When you move into a market, study your competitor's methods. Use his experience to avoid mistakes.

XI-22

Keep your people healthy. Save their energy. Cherish their morale. Do not overburden them unnecessarily. Carefully plan how to use your personnel. In this way, you will be prepared to take advantage of unexpected opportunities.

XI-23

Lead your organization where you want to go. Give your people no alternative—either they attain the goals you have set, or they fail completely. For if the only alternative is failure, what worthwhile person will not do his best to avoid it? When worthwhile people are committed, they do not fear failure. When they are focused on a common goal, they are calm. When they are deeply involved in their work, they have no choice but to succeed.

XI-24

Under these circumstances, worthwhile people stay alert. They follow procedures without supervision. They work hard without unnecessary promises or guarantees.

XI-25

On the day a major project is started, even worthwhile people may complain because they know how much work needs to be done.

XI-26

But when they find themselves with their backs up against the wall, they will exceed expectations because they are committed.

XI-27

You may ask: "Can people in my organization become committed and cooperative?" The answer is: Certainly. It is normal for people within the same organization to disagree. But throw them together into a lifeboat battered by a storm and they will help each other survive in the same way that the right hand helps the left.

XI-28

Once you are in command of competitive actions, you cannot depend on a large organization or abundant funding for your success.

XI-29

The goal of leadership is to make people work together to achieve desirable goals. A thorough understanding of the competitive situation will reveal how to manage both the weaker and stronger parts of your organization so that all can cooperate to achieve the goal.

XI-30
But cooperation among organizational members is essential to success. The effective executive creates a situation of cohesion through commitment in which he can command the whole organization as if he were commanding one person. He does this by planning his strategy in secret and managing its execution with clear and direct orders.

XI-31
He does not allow everyone in the organization to know the details of his plans. In this way, his competitor is not forewarned.

XI-32
He squelches speculation and kills rumors among his constituents. In this way, he maintains the focus and morale of his people.

XI-33
He changes direction and alters his methods. In this way, no one can anticipate his direction or destination.

XI-34
He modifies his positions and uses indirect approaches. In this way, his competitor does not understand the nature of his challenge until it is too late.

XI-35

The business of the executive in command is to bring his resources and people together and put them into a situation where they must commit to the success of his goals.

XI-36

He must put his organization into a position where the highest level of performance is necessary in order to succeed. He creates a situation where complete success or total failure are the only options. He pushes his organization forward and then burns the bridges behind it. There is no escape from commitment.

XI-37

He leads his organization up the ladder of high expectations, and when he decides the time is right, kicks away the ladder.

XI-38

In this way, although his organization does not know the details of his plans, when the executive asks them to perform, they obey as the sheep obey the shepherd.

XI-39

Do not ally with those who are unwilling to meet the challenge of competitive actions. Those who are unaware of the opportunities and obstacles are not competent to command an organization. Those who do not employ specialists and consultants cannot take advantage of their competitors' weakness nor react to unexpected circumstances. Those who are ignorant of how to maneuver in different competitive situations cannot be successful.

XI-40
When an effective executive moves into a competitor's territory, he does not allow his competitor to combine forces with his allies. He imposes his will on his competitor. He does not allow his competitor to rely on others for strength.

XI-41
Neither does he concern himself with conforming to folk wisdom. His desire for success is so strong that he worries only about using facts to produce effective results.

XI-42
When you lead, give rewards that no one else can give. Make plans that do not follow precedent. In this way, people will follow your vision. You will command the entire organization as if you were commanding a single person.

XI-43
Lead by example, not by words. Motivate people with the expectation of profit. Do not tell them about the risks involved. Put them into situations where they can choose either commitment or failure, nothing else. When worthwhile people face this choice, they will find the strength to win a victory.

XI-44
To create circumstances favorable to you, first pretend you are going along with your competitor's program.

XI-45
Make your competitor believe you are going in the direction he has determined for you. Lull him to sleep. In this way, when you execute your carefully developed plans, you can overcome your competition.

XI-46
From the moment competitive operations begin, maintain strict secrecy. Urge the policymakers to decide quickly, so you can act.

XI-47
When your competitor shows his weakness, move rapidly to take advantage of it. Seize what the competition values most. Make your competitor react in accordance with your timetable.

XI-48
Adapt your strategy according to the movements of the competition. Put yourself in a position to gain decisive shares of the market.

XI-49
Begin your actions quietly and secretly. When your competitor exposes his weakness, move quickly. In this way, your competitor will not be able to respond in time.

INCENDIARY ATTACKS

Sun Tzu said:

There are five objectives for attacks by fire: first, to burn personnel; second, to burn inventory; third, to burn equipment; fourth, to burn arsenals; fifth, to burn transportation. The equipment and material required for building a fire must be handy. Fires start best when the weather is dry and the constellations of the Sieve, the Wall, the Wings, and the Chariot are rising. Using fire to attack is smart. Using water to attack also gives you greater strength. But water can only divide or isolate the enemy; fire, on the other hand, can destroy him.

XII
Destroying Reputation

XII-1
Destroying a competitor's reputation is the least desirable and most dangerous competitive operation. It is, however, extremely effective. There are five areas which can be a focus for attacks on reputation: personnel or personal relationships; organizational products or individual performance; customers or employees; suppliers or supporters; and capital resources or financial backing.

XII-2
Your competitor must have a credible weakness that can be magnified or exposed before you can destroy his reputation.

XII-3
Further, the facts and resources necessary to carry out the task must already be at your disposal.

XII-4
Destroying reputation depends on the political and economic environment at the time. The political and eco-

nomic currents must carry the bad news effectively in order for the damage to spread.

XII-5
The appropriate time for starting a campaign to destroy a competitor's reputation is when there are other difficulties present on the political or economic scene. This is particularly true when there are problems within his constituency that have not yet found a convenient scapegoat.

XII-6
To destroy a competitor's reputation effectively, you must focus your attention on one of these five objectives and adapt your attack to meet the requirements of that objective.

XII-7
First, try to cause a credibility crisis within your competitor's most loyal constituents because this is the most effective method. If a crisis begins immediately, follow up quickly with pressure from outside. But if you cannot cause a crisis right away and your competitor remains calm, do not press your outside attack vigorously.

XII-8
Instead, let the campaign do as much damage as possible. As soon as a weakness or opportunity appears, then attack; otherwise, delay.

XII-9
If you determine that you should destroy a competitor's reputation and the timing is right, begin the campaign,

even if you must start outside his constituency. It is not always possible to get close enough to your competitor, particularly if he is clever.

XII-10
Attempting to destroy a competitor's reputation is a dangerous business. After you have started a destructive campaign, make sure you are not caught in the backdraft.

XII-11
Further, after the political and economic currents have flowed in a certain direction for a while, they will more than likely shift. Be prepared to modify your tactics or abandon the campaign if the time and current turn against you.

XII-12
All executives should be familiar with the five objectives of a campaign against reputation. Executives should be able to defend themselves or attack others in accordance with the strategic situation.

XII-13
Destroying reputation is a method of permanently defeating your competitor. Other methods of competition require great expenditures of resources and, even if successful, their results may not be permanent.

XII-14
A destroyed reputation, on the other hand, may cost you nothing more than a few well-placed words. More importantly, once destroyed, a reputation is hard to restore.

Sun Tzu said:

Do not attack your enemy unless you can profit from it. Do not consume resources unless there is a corresponding gain. Do not wage war unless you are in danger. A ruler should not raise an army out of rage. A commander should not attack the enemy out of anger or emotion. Move when it is profitable; stop when it is not. Therefore, an enlightened ruler is very prudent and a great commander is very cautious. By doing this, the state can be preserved and its defenses maintained.

XII-15

To defeat a competitor and take control of the situation without being able to benefit from victory is a misfortune. Competing for the sake of competition is a waste of time and resources, besides being an unwarranted risk.

XII-16

Therefore, a smart executive first weighs the benefits to be gained from mounting a particular challenge. Once he determines it is appropriate, he fights to win.

XII-17

Do not attack your competitor's reputation unless you can profit from it. Do not consume resources unless there is a corresponding gain. Do not act aggressively unless you are in danger.

XII-18

An executive should not compete out of emotion. He should not attack out of anger. Move when it is profitable; stop when it is not. While it is true that emotion can return to reason and anger to pleasure, it is also true that a destroyed reputation cannot be restored and a dead organization cannot be returned to life.

XII-19

Therefore, a smart executive acts wisely and cautiously. By doing this, his own weaknesses are minimized, his reputation is preserved, and his own organization remains intact.

Using Spies

Sun Tzu said:
A commander who takes advantage of war to gain personal fame and wealth, but does not spend money for information about the enemy, is inhumane. The reason enlightened rulers and competent commanders win victories, achieve outstanding successes, and surpass ordinary people is that they know critical information in advance. Intelligence comes only from people who know the enemy from personal experience. There are five types of intelligence activities: local intelligence, internal intelligence, counter intelligence, misleading intelligence, and continuing intelligence.

XIII
Gathering Intelligence

XIII-1
Investing resources for use in a specific competitive situation removes these resources from alternative uses. Money and manpower already committed to one conflict cannot be used for another.

XIII-2
Competitive actions may continue for many years while competitors attempt to position themselves for one decisive encounter. The reason smart executives win victories, achieve outstanding successes, and surpass others is that they know critical information in advance; that is, they know their competitor's objectives, resources, and activities. They know the minds of the targeted constituencies. Further, they win because they confuse the competition about their own intentions and circumstances.

XIII-3
This kind of critical advance information, or intelligence, is not provided by wishful thinking or speculation. It is not provided by examining past events or

activities. It is not provided by gathering, measuring, or analyzing marketplace or demographic data. Really useful intelligence comes from people who have first-hand knowledge and personal experience with the competition and constituents.

XIII-4

There two are goals for intelligence activities. The first goal is to obtain accurate, timely information about the objectives, resources, and activities of competitors and constituents. The second is to provide the competition with appropriately misleading information about your own objectives, resources, and activities. There are four sources that can be used to receive and transmit intelligence: general sources, internal intelligence, counterintelligence, and moles.

XIII-5

By combining these four sources of intelligence, no one can know how your information is obtained or provided. A powerful but mysterious network is created. This network is the most precious asset of the chief executive officer.

XIII-6

Local sources of intelligence are those that are easily accessed in the majority of industries. Local sources of intelligence include, for instance, people at industry conventions, low-level employees of the competition, trade publications, national publications and journals, manufacturers' representatives, and advertising. Local sources are good channels for disseminating misleading information to confuse the competition. But beware of rumors and folk wisdom yourself.

XIII-7
Internal sources of information are people working for or with the competition or important constituents who have access to important data. These sources are primarily executives and technical staff, but also include clerical people at lower levels who have access to critical information, particularly in companies with an unrestricted flow of information.

XIII-8
Counterintelligence agents are competition agents or moles within our company who have been converted to our use. They are the most valuable agents.

XIII-9
Remember that counterintelligence can be used by the competition, too. Some of your informants *are,* without a doubt, counteragents. When you discover a counteragent, *use him.* Provide the competition with misleading information. The counteragent will be believed without question for a time.

XIII-10
Moles are agents on our payroll who have regular jobs with constituents or competitors.

XIII-11
No activity is more closely tied to our success than effectively gathering and disseminating intelligence. No

reward should be greater than that given to those who provide essential intelligence. No operations should be more secret than those related to intelligence.

XIII-12
But only a supremely wise and superbly subtle executive can make effective use of intelligence.

XIII-13
The impact of intelligence is so pervasive, so encompassing and so universal that there is no activity where it cannot be put to use.

XIII-14
But it must be secret. If plans for gathering and disseminating intelligence are known, all involved are doomed to failure.

XIII-15
It does not matter what type of competitive actions are planned, or whose reputation is to be attacked; it is necessary to know the names of the executive involved, his assistants, his advisors, and even his driver. Informants and agents must provide this kind of information.

XIII-16
Converting the competition's own agents gives us a critical advantage. Therefore, we should lure them with profits, guide them, and protect them. In this way, they become part of our counterintelligence network.

XIII-17
An effective counterintelligence network gives us the

ability to judge the value of information provided by local sources and internal agents.

XIII-18
Because of counterintelligence, we can determine if misleading information has been effectively transmitted to the competition.

XIII-19
Because of counterintelligence, we can devise appropriate strategies for recruiting moles and protecting them from discovery. We can discover if our intelligence network has been compromised.

XIII-20
The chief executive officer must be aware of all aspects relating to intelligence activities. He must understand that counterintelligence is the most crucial element to success in competitive operations. He must understand that the reward for counterintelligence work should be extremely generous.

XIII-21
After all, the rise and fall of many executives and organizations is the direct result of the effective use of intelligence. Its importance cannot be ignored.

XIII-22
Smart executives employ only the most capable people in their intelligence networks. It is through these people that they achieve success. Intelligence is the essence and foundation of all competitive actions.

Appendix

Sun Tzu's Principles: A Summary

1. Learn to fight
2. Show the way
3. Do it right
4. Know the facts
5. Expect the worst
6. Seize the day
7. Burn the bridges
8. Do it better
9. Pull together
10. Keep them guessing

1. *Learn to fight.* Competition in life is inevitable. Further, competition occurs in all areas of life. Sun Tzu advises that we cannot learn too much about how to compete. On the other side of the issue, however, Sun Tzu warns against competition for its own sake. He notes that using competition simply to enrich oneself or to win without being able to benefit from the victory is risky and costly.

Competition should occur when we have something important to gain or when we are in danger. Further, in competitive situations, we should not allow our emotions to govern our actions. Emotion clouds reason and destroys objectivity, both of which are necessary for continuing competitive success. Loss of emotional control is a major handicap, as well as a damaging weapon in the hands of the competition.

2. ***Show the way.*** Sun Tzu tells us that leadership alone determines success. Leadership is a hot topic for business today. And, of course, it was just as important in ancient China. How might Sun Tzu define leadership? Confucius, who lived at the same time as Sun Tzu, taught a great deal about leadership in his analects. An analysis of Confucian teaching reveals that Confucius believed that effective leadership comes from seven characteristics: Self-discipline, Purpose, Accomplishment, Responsibility, Knowledge, "Laddership," and Example. (Many important leaders throughout ancient and modern history—Alexander, Caesar, Jesus Christ, Lincoln, Grant, Lee, Lawrence, Roosevelt, Patton, Marshall, and others—exhibit these seven characteristics.)

—*Self-discipline* means that a leader tends to live by a set of rules that he determines are appropriate for him and acceptable to his constituents. He does not need external motivation to ensure performance.

—*Purpose* means that a leader works to achieve objectives that are important to his constituents and does not constrain his goals with the narrow focus of strict self-interest.

—*Accomplishment* means that a leader defines results in terms of meeting the needs of his constituents.

—*Responsibility* means that a leader takes ownership of the outcomes of his decisions and actions.

—*Knowledge* means that a leader constantly strives to improve his understanding and ability.

—*Laddership* means that a leader works cooperatively with his constituents to reach agreed-upon objectives.

—*Example* means that a leader shows the way by his own actions.

Sun Tzu also mentions five character flaws that can lead to failure. These are recklessness, timidity, emotionalism, egoism, and overconcern for popularity.

3. ***Do it right.*** All competitive advantage is based on effective execution. Planning is important, but actions are the source of success. Without effective action, planning is a sterile exercise. Modern management theorists believe that a bias for action substantially improves chances for success.

Sun Tzu states that competitive advantage arises from creating favorable opportunities and then acting on these opportunities at the appropriate time. In other words, winners do the right things at the right moment.

But Sun Tzu also reminds us to govern the desire to act with the need for patience. He teaches us that we can be held responsible for putting ourselves in a position where we cannot be defeated, but others must create the opportunity to win. Hence, we must be willing to wait. Just because we know how to win does not mean we can win. Move when it is profitable and stop when it is not.

4. ***Know the facts.*** To achieve success, you must manage information. Information is the lifeblood of business. Sun Tzu says that information, or the lack of it, determines the probability of success. According to him, if sufficient reliable information is available, victory is certain. Sun Tzu teaches that there are two aspects to information management. One aspect is gathering information. The other aspect is giving it out. You gather information to make good decisions. You give out information to misdirect the competition. In either case, you must know the facts, or you will fail.

The best information comes from firsthand experience. Sun Tzu strongly champions the use of agents and informants to gather and transmit firsthand information. This may sound sinister; but, in fact, intelligence operations are both important and necessary. All organizations and individuals engage in intelligence operations to some extent or another. Wise organizations view intelligence operations as critical and invest the resources needed to make them pay off.

Sun Tzu warns us about relying on "folk wisdom." Folk wisdom is the body of unproven assumptions, unwarranted speculation, and generally accepted opinions that is present in any group of people. Great danger lies in not challenging folk wisdom. Reliable facts always precede successful actions.

Most decisions made during competitive activities have an element of uncertainty. We simply cannot know everything. Even so, decisions must be made. Sun Tzu tells us to consider everything and make our decisions by weighing the potential for success. That is, Sun Tzu is telling us to assess the probability of success before acting. Modern managers have access to a number of simple, but powerful, statistical techniques to assist them in quantifying uncertainty related to information. Deming and others have demonstrated that these techniques greatly improve the quality of decisions. Success on the information battlefield depends on knowing how to use and abuse statistics.

5. ***Expect the worst***. Sun Tzu issues a strong warning. Do not assume the competition will not attack. Rely, instead, on adequate preparation to defeat him. If you seek something that requires you to compete with someone else to obtain it, it is foolish to assume that person or organization is lying dormant. Of course, the competition is going to try to win the battle. Therefore, adequate preparation is necessary.

Sun Tzu issues another warning related to preparation. Do not tackle difficult problems when adequate resources are not available. Even with superior strategy, you will be defeated if you lack resources. According to Sun Tzu, it is not necessary to have the greatest number of men or the most money in order to succeed. What we must do is closely observe the competition and focus our resources on his weak spots. However, do not underestimate the competition. Consider carefully the meaning of his movements and tactics. Expect the worst in order to succeed.

6. ***Seize the day***. Quick victory is the aim of competitive action. The most important success factor in competition is speed. To win, do things the simple way whenever you can. Simple methods are effective and inexpensive. Try them first. If they do not work, you still have time to try something else. Staying one step ahead of the competition is worth more than any other advantage. When you are ahead, the competition must react.

Speed and innovation are the keys to staying ahead. Do simple things well. Do a lot of simple things very well, and you increase your chances of winning dramatically. This is particularly true if your competition believes that complexity breeds success. More often than not, complexity just breeds more overhead. Strategies that waste time and exhaust resources never work well. When water flows, it avoids the high ground and seeks the low ground. Successful strategies, likewise, avoid difficult methods and seek easy ones.

7. ***Burn the bridges***. When people are unified in their purpose, no obstacle can stand in their way. Sun Tzu advises the successful leader to place himself and his constituents in situations where they are in danger of failing. When people know they can fail if they do not work together, they will be unified in their purpose and will maintain their commitment to a set of goals and objectives. The successful leader pushes his constituents forward and then burns the bridges behind them.

Motivation and commitment are the keys to leadership. Sun Tzu tells us that people are motivated by the expectation of profit. When you face obstacles and challenges, focus the attention of your constituents on the benefits of success. Do not tell them about the risks involved, because this will demotivate them. To capture their attention, give them clearly defined goals and valuable rewards. Treat people well. Train them thoroughly. The success of the organization is built upon the individual success of its members.

8. **_Do it better_**. Sun Tzu says that in war there are only two types of tactics: expected and unexpected. Effective commanders combine expected and unexpected tactics according to the requirements of the situation. But it is unexpected tactics that create the opportunity for victory. Unexpected, or innovative, tactics cannot be defended against in advance. Innovation is the one weapon that makes you invincible. The power of innovation makes victory certain.

Effective innovation is not necessarily complicated or difficult. Successful TQM programs have shown the value of improving operations a little at a time. This goes back to the idea of doing simple things well. A corollary of this idea is to make simple improvements often. A large number of simple improvements can make a significant difference in performance. Those executives who are skillful at encouraging and implementing innovative ideas have infinite resources in a competitive situation.

9. **_Pull Together_**. Organization, training, and communication are the foundation of success. If you organize and train your constituents clearly, you will be able to control their actions in competition. If organization and training are vague, people cannot be relied on. They will fail you at the most critical moment. However, when expectations are clear

and organization structure is appropriate for their tasks, people will trust their leaders and follow them even under difficult circumstances.

Training is the essential element in getting people to pull together. The cost/benefit trade-off of effective training is huge when combined with appropriate organization and a reward system that does not demotivate people. Even though the benefits are obvious, most of what passes for training in corporate America is a total waste of time and resources. Why? Because it is boring! Training must be interesting in order to be effective.

Good training leads to common understandings and perceptions. Common understandings are essential for clear communication. This is particularly true during the heat of competition, when it is crucial to manage your constituents. Further, effective training builds constituent loyalty. Sun Tzu tells us that we cannot punish people until they feel loyalty to us; that is, until they consider themselves members of our constituent group. He also tells us that if we cannot punish people, we cannot control them.

Effective training keeps your constituents informed and promotes group comfort and stability. People who are comfortable and stable have healthier emotions and sharper minds. Keep your constituents healthy. Save their energy for important matters. Cherish their morale. Use your constituents carefully so they have reserve energy and capacity. In this way, you will be able to take advantage of unexpected opportunities and the leverage provided by innovation.

10. *Keep them guessing*. The best competitive strategies have no form. They are so subtle that neither the competition nor your constituents can discern them. If your strategy is a mystery, it cannot be counteracted. As a result, competitors will be forced to react after your strategy is

revealed. This gives you a significant advantage. As Sun Tzu says, "What does it matter if a competitor has greater resources? If I control the situation, he cannot use them." With control, victory can be crafted by those with skill. Even if the competition is strong, with control, you can make him lose his will to fight. Focus on your objective. Maintain control by keeping your strategies secret.

To get control, seize something your competitor wants or needs. When your competitor shows a weakness, move rapidly, without warning. Succeeding in a direct attack depends mainly on deception. The less a competitor knows about where you intend to focus your attention, the stronger you are. If he must prepare defenses at many points, because of limited resources, your competitor will be weak everywhere.